CHRISTMAS ANGELS

1 3 5 7 9 10 8 6 4 2

Square Peg, an imprint of Vintage
20 Vauxhall Bridge Road,
LONDON SW1V 2SA

Square Peg is part of the Penguin Random House group of companies
whose addresses can be found at global.penguinrandomhouse.com

Penguin
Random House
UK

First published by Square Peg in 2020

Penguin.co.uk/vintage

A CIP catalogue record for this book is available from the British Library

ISBN 9781529110364

Designed by Amy Lines
Photography by Lily Richards

Printed and bound in China

MIX
Paper from
responsible sources
FSC® C018179
www.fsc.org

Penguin Random House is committed to a
sustainable future for our business, our readers
and our planet. This book is made from Forest
Stewardship Council® certified paper.

CHRISTMAS ANGELS

Rowan Dobson

From lofty heights atop the trees
of homes around the world,
angels sit in front-row seats
whilst our Christmases unfurl.
With names and personalities,
they are just like family members,
who come to visit once a year
and stay throughout December.

They see us when we're sleeping,
(4pm in front of the box),
they know when we're awake
(4am up wrapping socks).
They hear the oven timer
telling us it's time to baste,

they sense old family tensions

and which gifts were bought in haste.

But like the snowflakes on our windows,

each angel is one of a kind;

with its story of arrival

to the home where it's enshrined.

Some are antiques passed through
the ages,

others have yet to fade,

some are meticulously constructed,

or haphazardly handmade.

Some bought without a second thought,

or almost thrown away,

what other household object

is treated in this way?

Forgotten for eleven months,

in lofts where they remain,

'til rediscovered and unboxed,

and admired once again.

Oh isn't she beautiful!

Where did you find her?

How ever was she made?

What's wrong with her eye?

Is she alright? She looks a bit decayed.

But isn't she sassy, isn't she fun,

treasured, timeless and twee,

despite her imperfections,

let's pop her on the tree!

This unusual, playful collection of portraits demonstrates the variety of styles, stories and personalities embodied by our favourite Christmas companions.

You will discover beloved angels who appear to epitomise the spirit of Christmas, and others who might be better suited to Halloween.

All kinds of tales accompany the portraits – car boot sale successes, clashes with household pets, house moves gone wrong, and perhaps most interestingly of all, details of how the angels were created and the sentimental value they behold.

Some have their quirks and foibles, but every single angel in this collection has the power to delight, confuse, spark a conversation or light up a room.

We hope you enjoy this extraordinary exploration.

BETTY

AGE *36*
HEIGHT *16 cm*
BELONGS TO *R. Yapp*
MATERIALS *Lace, satin, ribbon, cotton, plastic, faux hair, tinsel*

Sporting a strong fringe and pencilled-on eyebrows, Betty could be a modern-day style icon. A note for fashionistas: Bag yourself a cummerbund, ribbon and three petit pois ASAP. You saw it here first.

11

GERTIE

AGE *22*
HEIGHT *18 cm*
BELONGS TO *E. Steel*
MATERIALS *Wood, straw, plastic, ribbon, glitter, paper, metallic paint*

With the hairstyle of Norman Bates' mother, and a face without any features at all, some might say Gertie is more than a little frightening, but she has been cherished by the Steel household for over twenty years.

Presumably they operate under the mantra 'No features? No problem!'.

ANGEL MAE

AGE *Unknown*
HEIGHT *7 cm*
BELONGS TO *K. Kirkham*
MATERIALS *Clay*

Angel Mae was discovered in Sausalito, California, USA.

Even though she has the stance and knowing smirk of Mr Burns, she is described by her owner as 'feisty, super smart and good at gymnastics' – and judging by her hairstyle, she's also a Star Wars fan.

CAROL

AGE *28*
HEIGHT *20 cm*
BELONGS TO *C. Dobson*
MATERIALS *Lace, satin, ribbon, foil, plastic*

'Christmas Carol' – as she is known to friends – is from Hertfordshire, UK. What CC keeps beneath that huge skirt is a question she is asked often.

Well reader, we can reveal… it's just more skirt.

NELLIE

AGE *26*
HEIGHT *5 cm*
BELONGS TO *M. Stephenson*
MATERIALS *Wool, tinsel, ribbon*

Nellie was knitted many moons ago and gifted to the Stephenson family. She is very sweet, but very shy.

At parties it takes her a while to peek out from under her toupée, lower her scarf and engage in conversation. But once she does, she's full of surprisingly naughty jokes and quickly becomes the life and soul of any gathering.

IMOGEN

AGE 6
HEIGHT 9 cm
BELONGS TO T. Hill
MATERIALS Quality acid-free paper

Imogen came to life through the art of quilling, which involves cutting paper into long thin strips, rolling and pinching them into different shapes, and gluing the shapes together to make decorative art.

Her facial expression reflects the serene environment in which she was created.

21

HELEN

AGE *23*
HEIGHT *14 cm*
BELONGS TO *The Loughton Family*
MATERIALS *Paper, card*

Lovingly crafted using kirigami,
Helen is a reminder of the beauty
that can be created with a little
time and patience.

She was presented to the Loughton
family by a friend one frosty
December day, and has been
admired for many years since.

PEGGY

AGE *67*
HEIGHT *10 cm*
BELONGS TO *W. Salt*
MATERIALS *Felt, mesh, faux hair, plastic, cardboard*

The pre-Christmas party nerves got to Peggy a few hours prior to this photo being taken. She popped on her best gold mesh vest, had a few drinks to calm herself, before starting on her make-up… We've all been there.

Slightly sozzled, she went rogue with the rouge and will spend the rest of the evening swaying to whatever beat takes her fancy without a care in the world… until the morning, of course.

PATSY

AGE *68*
HEIGHT *9 cm*
BELONGS TO *W. Salt*
MATERIALS *Plastic, faux hair, cardboard, lace, mesh*

Patsy is Peggy's (see p. 25) slightly older, more responsible cousin. Both angels were created in the 1950s, and are purposefully kitsch.

Patsy swishes her Q-Tip wand in Peggy's general direction when she misbehaves and requires a little shooing along.

NICKY

AGE *46*
HEIGHT *20 cm*
BELONGS TO *C. Westaway*
MATERIALS *A vintage Mother of Pearl tourist bag from 1960s South Africa, a gorgeous brooch from the 1950s with a broken fastener*

Nicky's breath-taking attire will inspire celebrities all over the world to turn to upcycling for their next red carpet look.

FLORENCE

AGE *Unknown*
HEIGHT *16 cm*
BELONGS TO *S. Battley*
MATERIALS *Polyester, lace, clay*

Florence was found at a car boot fair in Somerset on a cold, wet morning in late winter.

Discarded and alone in a box on the floor, Florence was invited to make the Battley residence her new home, where she intends to stay for the foreseeable future.

MATILDA

AGE *40*
HEIGHT *17.5 cm*
BELONGS TO *The Dawes Family*
MATERIALS *Tinsel, mesh, foil, plastic*

Dressed to impress, Matilda's a real doll in her mesh gown and tinsel halo.

However, the Dawes family ask that we forgive her slightly crooked wings as 'Forty years of Christmas parties can have that effect!'.

JUDY

AGE *98*
HEIGHT *9 cm*
BELONGS TO *M. Ryles*
MATERIALS *Porcelain*

No danger of a monobrow here, Judy implores you to acknowledge her continual surprise at the small scale of her golden-tipped wings.

Her inability to fly rendered her destined to live a life of imprisonment inside a glass-fronted cabinet, only to be let free once in a generation as she is passed down through the Ryles family, transported from loft to loft.

PATRICIA

AGE *74*
HEIGHT *15 cm (volume included)*
BELONGS TO *A. Lines*
MATERIALS *Lace, tinsel, polyester, netting*

How many blow-dries is too many blow-dries? Pat has made it her life's mission to single-handedly redefine what we mean by a 'high volume bob'.

We can only assume her weekly request to the hairdresser is something like: 'Go big or go home – and leave the top wispy, unkempt and au naturel, darling'.

PARMINDER

AGE *22*
HEIGHT *13 cm*
BELONGS TO *H. Singh*
MATERIALS *Cork, cotton, nylon, mesh*

There's an optical illusion for you here.

Like the blue-black/white-gold dress of the internet, Parminder's face can be enjoyed in two ways: Her curtains can double-up as sunglasses, just like her eyelashes can be transformed into a moustache, creating a police detective-esque alter-ego that only comes out when the Singh family are firmly asleep.

NOOR

AGE *14*
HEIGHT *10 cm*
BELONGS TO *H. Campana-Frost*
MATERIALS *Banana leaves, sisal*

Handmade in Kenya from banana leaves and sisal, Noor is depicted deep in prayer.

Her name means 'happy' or 'cheery', so she can be relied upon year after to year to bring peace, cheer and goodwill to any household.

TALLULAH

AGE *Doesn't believe in age, but believes in energy*
HEIGHT *6 cm*
BELONGS TO *D. Hobday*
MATERIALS *Felt, wool, polyester, tinsel*

Who needs eyelashes, eyebrows, or a nose, when you have a face, dreads and a sense of inner calm like Tallulah?

Namaste.

BRENDA

AGE *54*
HEIGHT *7 cm*
BELONGS TO *V. Brown*
MATERIALS *Clay*

Should there be a demand for a stop-motion recreation of popular British children's TV show *Postman Pat*, Brenda would be a shoe-in for a supporting role.

We'll keep everything crossed for a Christmas special, Bren.

RHONDA

AGE *12*
HEIGHT *14 cm*
BELONGS TO *C. Power*
MATERIALS *Plastic, card, lace*

Since returning home from a car boot sale eleven years ago, Rhonda had been engaged in a feud with the Power family dog.

Benny the beagle would spend hours at the base of the Christmas tree growling ever so softly – it was almost imperceptible to the human ear – but Rhonda could always hear him.

Benny sadly passed away this October, so we know who won that war...

PEARL

AGE *20*
HEIGHT *6 cm*
BELONGS TO *E. Greaves*
MATERIALS *Cotton, felt, hessian, beads, a button*

Another upcycled creation, Pearl was formed using treasured fabrics from a baby's first dress, as well as silk left over from a wedding dress and christening gown, combined with some hessian to form the rustic, timeless look you see before you.

GABRIEL

AGE *82*
HEIGHT *4.5 cm*
BELONGS TO *D. Addison*
MATERIALS *Porcelain*

A lifelong choirboy, Gabriel takes Christmas carols seriously.

He can be seen here bellowing 'Five Go-o-ld Rings' with all the might he can muster, and suggests you join in at the next chorus.

CHERIE

AGE *27*
HEIGHT *14 cm*
BELONGS TO *A. Prideaux*
MATERIALS *Card, beads*

Cherie was created as an homage to Cher.

There's no need to turn back time with this ageless classic. Cherie fittingly models a billowing dress with angel sleeves.

We have been informed that her beaded wings are in the shape of a heart as a reminder of both the meaning of Christmas, and the 2017 Billboard Music Awards, where Cher wore a heart-shaped nipple sticker.

LEWIS, DIANA & TESSA

AGE *7, 35, 6*
HEIGHT *6 cm, 9 cm, 6 cm*
BELONGS TO *March Muses*
MATERIALS *Polymer clay*

When Alison Burton and Natalie Duvall struggled to find figurines of colour to decorate their homes with, they decided to make their own.

Named after an inspirational person of colour who shares their birth month, Lewis, Diana & Tessa spread Christmas cheer and empowerment in equal measure.

PETER

AGE *8*
HEIGHT *9 cm*
BELONGS TO *J. Paramor*
MATERIALS *Glass*

Despite being bought just for Christmas, Peter is on display throughout the year because he is loved so very much.

Everybody who makes his acquaintance agrees there is something magical about him, and it would be shame to box him up for eleven months of the year.

Amen to that.

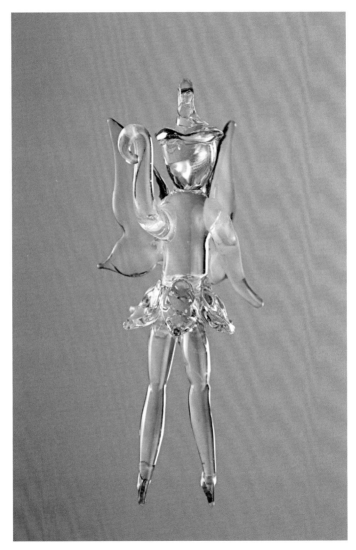

IMANI AND IMAYA

AGE *4*
HEIGHT *5.5 cm*
BELONGS TO *Mark*
MATERIALS *Recycled newspaper*

These crowned beauties are made
by extremely talented artisans in
Sri Lanka.

Newspaper is used to prove
that a sustainable alternative
material to plastic can be just as
artistically effective, without causing
unnecessary damage to our planet.

Greta would be proud.

POLLY AND PENNY

AGES *6 and 40*
HEIGHT *6 cm and 9 cm*
BELONGS TO *S. Earnshaw*
MATERIALS *Wood, beech, acrylic paint*

Polly and Penny are here to remind us how good mother-daughter twinning hairstyles can look – particularly those involving golden hippie headbands.

They searched high and low for matching glasses, but struggled to find frames wide enough.

If you lean in a bit closer, you might be able to sense the air of dissatisfaction (which inevitably comes from a failed shopping trip) emanating from this portrait.

NATALIE

AGE 7
HEIGHT *14 cm*
BELONGS TO *B. Batke*
MATERIALS *Satin ribbon, beads, plastic*

Natalie was created using the Japanese kanzashi technique, which is the art of intricately folding fabric into shapes which resemble a flower.

Natalie's dress and wings are made up of over one hundred folded 'petals'.

Quite understandably, some of the other angels in this collection refused to feature on the pages either side of Natalie for fear of being overshadowed.

THE NAPIER SISTERS

AGE *94*
HEIGHT *11 cm*
BELONGS TO *L. Barrett*
MATERIALS *Clay*

This trio belonged to a lady called
Mrs Napier who lived in Esher, UK.
Feeling neglected by her family,
Mrs N left everything she owned to
her decorator.

Feeling flattered (and probably a little
bewildered), the decorator took 'The
Napier Sisters' to a car boot sale. He
refused to separate them, and would
only accept an offer for the set, thus
saving any unnecessary emotional
turmoil for all involved.

DONNA

AGE *19*
HEIGHT *11 cm*
BELONGS TO *S. Sandon*
MATERIALS *Plastic, polyester*

Dominating the collection and whipping the Sandon family into shape, Donna proves that what an angel lacks in wings, can be made up for in sass, style and a mildly threatening demeanour.

She is deployed atop the tree, ready to pounce and suggest a suitable penalty should anybody be caught cheating during charades.

SUNNY

AGE *2*
HEIGHT *8.5 cm*
BELONGS TO *J. Swales*
MATERIALS *Felt, beads, wool*

Made as an example to share with stitching group 'Stitch & Stuff', Sunny possesses a variety of stitches: blanket, variegated blanket, feather and beaded.

Her creator got so carried away they stitched in Sunny's arms, so she is destined to be swaddled for eternity.

Lucky thing.

SHEILA

AGE *44*
HEIGHT *16 cm*
BELONGS TO *B. Coates*
MATERIALS *Plastic, netting, tinsel, shoelaces*

With the head of a doll, a fascinator body and suede shoelace legs, Sheila immediately inspires one question: 'What happened?'.

When asked for her backstory, the Coates family refused to comment, which to us, says it all.

CARINA

HEIGHT *10.5 cm*
BELONGS TO *C. Andersen*
MATERIALS *Felt and 100% polyester toy stuffing*

Carina is from Denmark – hence why she looks so content.

Who knew that pairing a gold halo with rose-gold wings would have such stunning results? The Scandi's knew – they always know.

ASHA

AGE *3*
HEIGHT *10 cm*
BELONGS TO *K. Vadher*
MATERIALS *Cotton, tulle, merino wool, feathers*

As a British Asian born and brought up in London, Kiren wanted an angel to reflect her and her daughters, but struggled to find one.

She created Asha, who now makes her daughters' eyes light up any time she's in the room.

NEVE

AGE 5
HEIGHT *15 cm*
BELONGS TO *A. Jhita*
MATERIALS *Wire, thread, silk flowers, feathers, wool, ribbon, beads*

Delicately constructed, Neve would brighten any mediocre tree.

She is the 'ice princess' of the Jhita family, and ensures everybody remains cool, calm and collected over the Christmas period.

ELIZABETH

AGE 62
HEIGHT 15 cm
BELONGS TO R. Boscawen
MATERIALS Plastic, polyester

The moment the camera flashed, Elizabeth raised her right hand to her cheek in horror, as it dawned on her that she'd left the oven on.

Mere seconds later she could be seen dashing across the studio carpark yelling 'I hope the Boscawens like their turkey dry!'.

As luck would have it, they do.

GEORGIE

AGE *33*
HEIGHT *7 cm*
BELONGS TO *L. Finch*
MATERIALS *Felt, plastic, tinsel, mesh, horse hair*

Bought in 1987, the Finch family believe Georgie symbolises the end of a Christmas Eve night out on the town.

Eyelashes falling off, lipstick smeared across her cheek, hair caught up in her tiara, Georgie's open arms seek a trusted friend to take her home, preferably via a kebab shop.

EMMA

AGE 6
HEIGHT 17 cm
BELONGS TO A.M. Ailoae
MATERIALS Tinsel, ribbon, felt, cotton

Emma and her sister Ella (see p.85), were both handcrafted by the extremely talented Andreea.

The folded ribbons create a solid yet delicate layered base, as well as a dashing Elizabethan-style neck ruff.

It's couture, darling.

ELLA

AGE 6
HEIGHT *17 cm (tallest side)*
BELONGS TO *A.M. Ailoae*
MATERIALS *Ribbon, felt, cotton, beads*

Had we decided to create an award for 'the angel who best embodies a famous landmark', Ella would have won it hands down.

But can you name that landmark?

Clue: It rhymes with 'The cleaning power of geezers'.

JOSEPHINE

AGE *22*
HEIGHT *5 cm*
BELONGS TO *H. Adam-Smith*
MATERIALS *Wool*

Hattie kindly knitted this angel as a gift for her friend, only to find it back in her own home a year later.

Hattie's 'friend' made the outrageous claim that she 'just fancied having a star this year instead'. That was twenty years ago.

Hattie is still fuming and plans to give her a copy of this book to tell her so.

DAPHNE

AGE *56*
HEIGHT *13 cm*
BELONGS TO *R. Cugnoni*
MATERIALS *Plastic, netting, wire, beads*

Every Christmas Day, the Cugnoni family have a portrait taken in front of the tree. Daphne is always delighted to see she is the only one who doesn't appear to age.

What she doesn't realise however, is that the family are terrified of where that red-hot candle will end up should they capture Daphne's bad side, and so rely heavily on Photoshop every year to save their skins.*

*Daphne has been edited here too. Luckily, she can't read, so will never know. Please refrain from reading this aloud should you find yourself in her company.

BEE

AGE *34*
HEIGHT *14 cm*
BELONGS TO *T. Sealy*
MATERIALS *Plastic, ribbon, wool*

Thanks to a house move – always a dangerous activity for a Christmas angel – the Sealy family searched high and low but Bee couldn't be found.

After accepting their terrible loss and making do with a cheap, low-quality alternative (who understandably didn't make the cut for this collection), Bee was found a decade later in the loft amongst a bin bag of Beanie Babies.

Bee said of the ordeal: 'What the Beanie Babies lacked in personality, they made up for in cushioning... Honestly, I'm fine. Please stop fussing'.

THE DERRY SISTERS

AGE *17*
HEIGHT *4.5 cm*
BELONGS TO *D. Addison*
MATERIALS *Card, foil*

This gorgeous Irish girl gang have mastered the 'click and sway' motion that every successful pop group must perfect. However, Orla at the back is just slightly out of time.

There is always one…

CHRISTA

AGE *46*
HEIGHT *8 cm*
BELONGS TO *S. Potter*
MATERIALS *Felt*

Bought in Boots in 1974, Christa was a special gift for Sarah's first Christmas from her mother.

Recently named after Sarah's father, Christopher, who passed away in 2018, Christa is now her own angel. She now lives in the cupboard since his star has replaced her on the tree.

If she looks a little smoke damaged, it's because she survived a chimney fire. We think she's beautiful just the same.

AGNES

AGE *52*
HEIGHT *9 cm*
BELONGS TO *H. Walker*
MATERIALS *Plastic*

The Walker family love a sing-song, but Agnes tends to go a little off-piste with both the lyrics and tune.

She has been persuaded to carry the songbook at all times, but she'll be damned if they think she's going to look at it.

All she wants for Christmas, is to jam.

LIZA

AGE *57*
HEIGHT *12 cm*
BELONGS TO *L. Barrett*
MATERIALS *Plastic, felt, polyester*

Liza can be seen modelling one
of her twelve outfits here. She has
the most versatile wardrobe of the
collection.

This one is what she calls her 'Elton
John number'. No news yet on how
Elton feels about that.

ROBERT

AGE *63*
HEIGHT *6 cm*
BELONGS TO *L. Williams*
MATERIALS *Felt, tinsel, wood*

You might think you're looking at Robert's face, but that is in fact his chin. He's a direct descendant of ghost-muppet Jacob Marley (of *Muppet Christmas Carol* fame).

Sadly Robert has never been able to see the film – thanks to his hat.

OLIVIA

AGE 5
HEIGHT 6 cm
BELONGS TO N. Genney
MATERIALS Cotton and wood,
(she's eco and vegan friendly)

Nici made this for her daughter who loves 'fairies, angels and anything miniature'.

Olivia wears the crocheted winged onesie really well. So well in fact that we're going to order one ourselves. Why not pop one on your Christmas list too?

That'd be lovely.

LITTLE KASIA

AGE *1*
HEIGHT *4.5 cm*
BELONGS TO *K. Niklas*
MATERIALS *Wool*

Another crocheted delight, Little Kasia is one of a set of six made by Kasia for each of her three children.

One of the smallest angels of the collection at just 4.5 cm, there is something wonderfully understated about Little Kasia, but we get the distinct impression she shouldn't be underestimated.

ELLIE

AGE *25*
HEIGHT *6.5 cm*
BELONGS TO *K. Neilan*
MATERIALS *Cotton, ribbon, lace, wool*

We don't know what it is about Ellie
– perhaps her stuffing, her sweet
smile, her open arms or her modest,
timid nature – but we think she is the
warmest, most cuddliest angel of
the collection.

The Neilan family think so too – she
has sat atop the tree in their porch
for over twenty-five consecutive
Christmases, welcoming friends,
family and carol singers alike with the
same sunny temperament.

SUZIE

AGE *22*
HEIGHT *12 cm*
BELONGS TO *L. Barrett*
MATERIALS *Plastic, faux hair, tinsel*

Suzie's halo handily doubles up as a tambourine.

Suzie arrived with a note from The Barretts to say 'She's very talented, but when we have our backs turned, she likes to sneak up behind us, bang her tambourine and scurry up the tree. It was actually quite amusing the first time…'.

MARÍA JESÚS GARCÍA DE LA FUENTE

AGE *17*
HEIGHT *12.5 cm*
BELONGS TO *F. Wilson*
MATERIALS *Plastic, faux hair*

María was discovered by the Wilson family in a holiday villa in Spain.

Caught mid-twirl here, María often glares down from the top of the tree. She doesn't say anything, but her eyes yell 'WHY AREN'T YOU DANCING? PUT THAT MINCE PIE DOWN AND GET UP!'.

BILLY

AGE 5
HEIGHT 14 cm
BELONGS TO *The Porters*
MATERIALS *Card, tinsel*

Christmas is a time of reflection – a sentiment aptly embodied by this conical character.

But do you see Billy's headwear as a modernist crown or a tuft of auburn hair? Your answer reflects more than you might think…

MELISSA

AGE *31*
HEIGHT *10 cm*
BELONGS TO *J. Cole*
MATERIALS *Beads, string*

Cleverly constructed using hundreds of beads, Melissa comes into her own when the Coles switch on the lights of the tree and settle down to watch a Christmas film.

Melissa can be seen glistening in the corner as her beads reflect the many bulbs of the fairy lights, throwing the most marvellous shapes onto the surrounding walls.

DOLLY

AGE *10*
HEIGHT *7.5 cm*
BELONGS TO *M. Harper*
MATERIALS *Tinsel, cotton, brass*

The reason why Dolly is looking a little sheepish, is because she has just woken up the Harper household – as she does every December morning – with what she calls her 'festive fanfare'.

LINDSAY

AGE *36*
HEIGHT *12.5 cm*
BELONGS TO *L. Foley*
MATERIALS *Plastic, felt, card*

Lindsay models a glorious golden bib here, which she uses to catch the crumbs of her Christmas dinner.

She likes to pick at the remnants after her afternoon doze, then swiftly get stuck into dessert.

TAYLOR

AGE *24*
HEIGHT *5.5 cm*
BELONGS TO *K. Swift*
MATERIALS *Card*

Kate made Taylor whilst in primary school over twenty years ago. She is adored by the Swift family, but she is a point of annual contention: is her smile sweet and innocent or is it a little too knowing?

Thoughts on a postcard.

PIP

AGE *12*
HEIGHT *5 cm*
BELONGS TO *C. Perry*
MATERIALS *Beads, string*

Aztec-inspired Pip is the Perry family's golden good luck charm. When not adorning the tree, she is hooked to a set of cupboard keys where Father Christmas hides his early deliveries.

She can hardly wait for Christmas morning to come when the presents are finally revealed.

RENATE

AGE *17*
HEIGHT *18 cm*
BELONGS TO *All The Hearts
She Touches*
MATERIALS *Plastic*

Don't be misled by her ice-like
complexion – Renate is far from frosty.

When viewed in the light of a roaring
fire, the delicacy of her dazzling attire
comes to life. Combined with her
majestic grace, it's crystal clear to see
why she melts hearts.

ACKNOWLEDGEMENTS

Thank you to all the contributors who sent in their angels and shared their stories with us – we really couldn't have made this book happen without you.

Thank you to Lily Richards for her stunning photographs which brought each angel to life, and to Amy Lines for her dazzling design. Thanks also to Rowan Yapp, Harriet Dobson and Mireille Harper for their editorial support and enthusiasm.

We would like to thank the following for their angel contributions:

Beata Batke | Owner of Natalie | Founder of ATB Art Craft

Clare Power | Owner of Rhonda | Founder of Carry On Retro

Charlotte Andersen | Owner of Carina | Founder of Scandinavian Design

Francesca Dawes | Owner of Matilda

Harriet Walker | Owner of Agnes

Jo Swales | Owner of Sunny | Founder of Stitch and Stuff

Katarzyna Niklas | Owner of Little Kasia

Kiren Vadher | Owner of Asha | Founder of Little Star and Sun

Lorraine Williams | Owner of Robert

Alison Burton and Natalie Duvall | Owners of Lewis, Diana and Tessa | Founders of March Muses

Michelle Ryles | Owner of Judy

Sally Battley | Owner of Florence | Founder of Maltress Trading

Sarah Potter | Owner of Christa

Charlie Westaway | Owner of Nicky | Founder of The Indie Folk

Tracey Hill | Owner of Imogen | Founder of Pretty Paper Art By Tracey

Hannah Campana-Frost | Owner of Noor | Founder of Wild Home Online

Mark | Owner of Imani and Imaya | Founder of By Amber and Rose

Wendy Salt | Owner of Peggy and Patsy | Founder of Fetch and Sow Vintage

Eve Greaves | Owner of Pearl | Founder of Mirabelle Embroidery

Andreea Mihaela Ailoae | Owner of Emma and Ella

Stephanie Earnshaw | Owner of Polly and Penny | Founder of Gabe and Penny

Jordan Paramor | Owner of Peter

Louise Barrett | Owner of The Napier Sisters, Suzie and Liza

Dawn Addison | Owner of The Derry Sisters and Gabriel | Founder of Pretty Vintage House

Leah Finch | Owner of Georgie

Nici Genney | Owner of Olivia | Founder of Olieve

Debi Hobday | Owner of Tallulah | Founder of Debi.Lou

Amandeep Jhita | Owner of Neve | Founder of Craft Celebration UK

Freya Wilson | Owner of María

And to everyone at VINTAGE who also shared their angels with us.